SNIFF-SNUFF-SNAP!

Lynley Dodd.

Spindlewood

The sun was hot,
the day was still,
the animals came
to drink their fill.
Down past rocks
and thornbush tree,
down to the waterhole,
one
two
three.

One bossy warthog,
tail up high,

Two yellow weaver birds,
passing by.
'EEEEEEE!'
squealed the warthog,
'SNIFF-SNUFF-SNAP!'
He chased them away …
BUT

they both
sneaked
back.
Back to the waterhole,
green and brown
and slowly,
the water went down
and
down.

Three shy dik-diks,
tip-tap-toe,
four old baboons
in a grumpy row.
'EEEEEEE!'
squealed the warthog,
'SNIFF-SNUFF-SNAP!'

He chased them away ...
BUT

they all
sneaked
back.
Back to the waterhole,
green and brown
and slowly,
the water went down
and
down.

Five fine leopards,
out of sight,
six striped zebras,
black and white.
'EEEEEEE!'
squealed the warthog,
'SNIFF-SNUFF-SNAP!'

He chased them away ...
BUT

they all
sneaked
back.
Back to the waterhole,
green and brown
and slowly,
the water went down
and
down.

Seven tall giraffes
with feet astride,
eight fat elephants,
side by side.
'EEEEEEE!'
squealed the warthog,
'SNIFF-SNUFF-SNAP!'

He chased them away …
BUT

they all
sneaked
back.
Back to the waterhole,
green and brown
and slowly,
the water went down
and
down.

Back came the warthog,
tired and hot,
for a long,
cool drink
at his favourite spot.
Down past rocks
and thornbush tree,
he came to the waterhole
BUT
what did he see?